JOHN COLET

A Preacher
To Be
Reckoned With

Colet's 'preferred forum was... the pulpit'

John B.Gleason

DAVID H.J.GAY

First published by BRACHUS 2011

Scripture quotations, unless otherwise stated,
are from the New King James Version

INTRODUCTION

It is the late fifteenth century. The medieval Roman Church, collapsing under the weight of its own corruption, has, thus far, resisted calls from within for serious reformation, and resisted with barbaric cruelty. John Wycliffe has been dead for a hundred years, his bones having been burned in 1427, and Lollardy has been crushed (yet not exterminated – 'heresy' simmers just beneath the surface). But Rome has more to contend with than internal pressures for reform. Christendom is besieged by an enemy from the east and south. The consequences of the papal schism have so weakened the papacy that the decadent Church is impotent in the face of the persistent and growing threat of Islam. So much so, Christendom has been banished to the north-western extremity of the known world, the Church long since having been driven out of Africa by the warring hordes of Mohammed, his followers then moving on into Spain – where, for seven hundred years, they have kept their hold. Constantinople fell to the Saracen in 1453. Venice and Rome are threatened. And Christendom has suffered all this, despite the treasure in blood and gold which it has lavished on the Crusades. In the late fifteenth century, Islam can boast five times – five times – as many adherents as Christianity. Christianity is doomed.

Or so it must have seemed.

But... But God...

God does not *need* mortals – but he usually chooses to work through men and women to accomplish his purposes. So it was in the late fifteenth century. One of the men God used at that time is the man I want to speak to you about – John Colet.

I do not wish to be misunderstood. I am far from endorsing everything Colet stood for, everything he said and wrote. Far from it, I say. Colet was a man of his time. Yes, of course. But, having said that, I still have big reservations. He was born, lived and died a Roman Catholic. He was fascinated with the writings of Pseudo-Dionysius the Areopagite. True, these works severely rebuke Church scandals, they do nothing to support the Roman sacerdotal system, and they teach that baptism and the Lord's supper are symbols of an inward work and not conveyors of sacramental grace. Nevertheless, taken as a whole, their mystical speculations on such things as 'the celestial hierarchies', and their defective view of Christ's atonement, leave them – and Colet – open to heavy criticism. Moreover, I deplore Colet's acceptance of several simultaneous absentee preferments (paid posts within the Church). I find it strange, also, that he is listed among the judges of the Lollards who suffered under Archbishop Warham in 1511.

I do not, therefore, intend to indicate approval of Colet in every particular. But the same could be said if I was writing about Martin Luther or John Calvin, to take but two. And Oliver Cromwell had his warts. Not everything they did, said and wrote was right and good. Far from it. Nevertheless, I still can – and do – respect them and their works, and can see how God used them in furthering his cause. I can draw lessons from their lives – lessons we desperately need to learn today. The same goes for John Colet.

Coming to it from the opposite direction, I do not want to perpetuate the 19th century myth – which owes its origin and development largely to Frederic Seebohm's *The Oxford Reformers*, first published in 1867, and brought out in J.M. Dent's *Everyman's Library* in 1914 – that Colet was the Reformation's John the Baptist. Nor do I turn to Colet for his scholarship. No! But I do write about John Colet because, for all his shortcomings, he was a great preacher. The pulpit was his speciality, his province; it was not the scholar's desk or academic's lectern. That is how he saw it himself. He was a preacher. Not only that, he was – what should be a given, but, sadly, too often it is not – a *decided* preacher. Colet was no fence-sitter.

In saying that he was a preacher first and foremost, I am not suggesting that Colet was devoid of scholarship. Not at all. But, I emphasise, he was primarily a preacher. He knew that it is only spiritual men who will ever come to understand Scripture, to grasp what God is saying to us in his word. It is not a question of learning. All the learning, all the study in the world, will never lead a man to truly see the meaning of Scripture. It needs the Holy Spirit's power to illuminate the mind and heart. Even so, Colet knew that God usually uses a preacher in bringing this about.

It is also important to remember that Colet distinguished between the commentator and the interpreter. While both start with the text of Scripture, *that* is where the commentator finishes. Having got at the text, however, the preacher is determined to apply it to his hearers. He knows the text is not the end in itself. The text has to come off the page, it has to live, it has to reach the mind, the heart and the life of those who hear. The preacher knows that he must do what he can, under the impulse of God's Spirit, to make the text speak to men, and to move them to obedience. This is what the preacher sets out to do, this is what he wants to do.

And this is what made Colet tick. In short, I say it again, Colet was a preacher, and no run-of-the-mill preacher at that! Now the world is ever in need of great preachers and great preaching – 'great' in the right sense. Never more so than today! That is why I have produced this little work. I hope it will encourage all who value the powerful preaching of the gospel of Christ.

COLET'S LIFE AND WORK

John Colet was born in 1466 or 7, the eldest son of the Lord Mayor of London. Graduating at Oxford in 1490, he travelled on the Continent from 1493 to 1496, where, greatly impressed with the 'new learning' of the humanists, he had the courage to turn his back on the hair-splitting logic of the scholastics which had dominated the medieval Church for centuries.

The scholastics? The scholastics, or Schoolmen, of the medieval universities, who flourished between the 12th and 16th centuries, sought to arrive at 'truth' by disputation and drawing endless distinctions, with the aim of reconciling Scripture and pagan philosophy. Thomas Aquinas' *Summa Theologica* (1265–1274), in which he cited Scripture, Greek philosophers, the Fathers, Jews and Muslims, is considered to be the pinnacle of the scholastic system. Under the principles of the Schoolmen, theology students of the day were taught, and had to master, Peter Lombard's *Sentences* – a massive compilation of Scripture and the Fathers, written in 1150. All the leading medieval theologians had studied and commentated on this scholastic work.

Colet, sailing against wind and tide, broke entirely with this. On his return to England in 1496, he settled in Oxford and announced a series of lectures to which he invited all, free of charge. What did he choose for the subject of his lectures? Paul's letter to the Romans.

But it was not only the choice of subject which was new. After all, the Schoolmen studied Scripture. But in what way did they study the sacred oracles? It was Colet's *approach* to Paul's letter to the Romans which so radically differed from that of the scholastics.

Rejecting secular scholarship and pagan philosophy, Colet turned his back on the scholastic method of interpreting Scripture. He had no time for Aquinas who, he said, had 'contaminated the teaching of Christ with his profane philosophy'.

As a result, Colet did not treat Paul's letter as a collection of isolated texts upon which to deliver a series of dry, detached and threadbare philosophisings drawn from the Schoolmen and the Fathers. Rather, he argued out the letter to the Romans as a whole, bringing out the practical meaning of the apostle's words as addressed to the first century believers at Rome. Colet wanted to get at – as he put it, 'dig out, unearth, bring out, hammer out, draw forth' – and deliver the drift and sense of the entire book. He wanted to open up Paul's meaning to his hearers. Moreover, it was not theoretical logic which interested Colet, but the practical benefit of the application of Paul's teaching to those gathered before him. He wanted them to see the fruits of the doctrine of Romans in their day-to-day lives. And in their eternal state.

And he had hearers. Colet's audacity, and the novelty of his subject and style, ensured an audience; abbots, doctors, priests – men of all kinds – attended him. At the start, some came because they were curious. Some came to find fault. But Colet overcame their questions and their doubts. They came again and again, coming now to learn, bringing their notebooks with them. They found in Colet an able, fluent teacher who spoke not merely with his lips, but with and from his heart, and, moreover, spoke to *their* hearts through their minds. He reached them. He communicated with them. Above all, he communicated *to* them the thrilling message of the gospel as discovered in the letter to the Romans. His hearers found reality and life – not the cold, dry, boring, tortuous philosophy of the *Sentences* as endlessly served up in the schools. Colet's zeal warmed his hearers' hearts. Not only so. Their lives were changed as they were brought under Colet's power in applying Paul's argument in the Romans.

I am not claiming that Colet got as close to the heart of Romans as Luther would within a few years, but it was Colet's approach to the apostle's book, and what he *did* discover in it, that I want to emphasise. *This* is the point.

Colet's lectures were so effective, they started a chain reaction of such energy that within forty years the *Sentences* were banned from Oxford, and Lombard's discarded leaves were allowed to blow around the quadrangles as so much waste paper, fit only to be picked up and used to mark the fences needed to keep the deer within the woods for the benefit of huntsmen.

Having admitted Colet's failure to reach the full meaning of Romans, I do not want to give the wrong impression the other way, however. He was very clear that the Old Testament was preparatory for Christ; that Moses and David spoke of Christ; that old-covenant shadows point to Christ. As for the law, because of the sinner's weakness and inability to keep it, Colet rightly argued that it never made any sinner right with God. He said such things as: 'Whatever Moses wrote pertains to Christ'. 'The meaning of the holy Scriptures is spiritual through and through, all of which Jesus made clear to his followers'. 'Christ is the rock who steadfastly endures and, when struck on the cross, poured forth life-giving blood that satisfies thirst for all eternity'. Colet was in no doubt that the church was redeemed by the blood which flowed from the side of Christ. As I say, although he did not reach Luther's understanding of Romans, he wasn't so very far off.

One night in the winter vacation of 1496-7, a priest – who was attending Colet's lectures – knocked on Colet's door. Gathering close round the fire, the two men talked. And talked. Somewhat embarrassed, the priest cautiously drew a manuscript from the folds of his garment. It was the letters of Paul written out in his own hand, he said. The two men warmed to each other as they discussed the apostle's doctrine. Comparing Colet's method with that of the scholastics, the priest asked his teacher for some hints as to how he himself might best get the marrow out of Paul. Colet responded at once. Turn up the first chapter of Romans, he urged, turn it up. Colet began to speak. The priest, fearing he might forget, said he would write down the spontaneous thoughts as Colet uttered them. The list rapidly lengthened. Later, Colet, writing to the Abbot of Winchcombe, enclosed this list of his comments on the opening chapter of Romans. And he took the unusual step of asking for the return of his letter with the comments – he did not want to lose them, he explained, but thought of leaving them behind after his death for others to read as a memorial to him. From such little acorns, big oaks grow.

It is worthwhile pausing for a moment to listen to Colet speaking in that letter:

Faith in Christ comes from a calling by grace... It is for the preacher of God's word to teach all men. At no time, in no place, and in no way, must one be ashamed of the gospel. A powerful justification of men by God is shown in the gospel. The just man is the man who believes and trusts in God, while the man who trusts in created things of any sort is impious and unjust; whence it follows that just-ness is confidence in God, while trust in others is unjust-ness, connected with a lack of trust in God. What applies to faith applies also to the worship of God. To trust in anyone other than God is idolatry... The ultimate impiety is the neglect of God; those that neglect God are neglected by him, and, neglected by God, they perish in numberless ways. From a perverse will arises unnatural perversion. Along with sin, the punishment of sin – its wages – grows too. The last end of sin is eternal death, which sinners deserve... It is up to the man who knows the right way to point it out to others, and unceasingly summon them back to it...

Colet went on:

[I] garnered these thoughts from the first chapter of the letter to the Romans, and set them down right away. Nor are these the only ones that could have been noted. From the salutation, for example, others may be gathered: that Christ was promised in the revelations of the prophets; that Christ sanctifies men, and through Christ is the resurrection of both their souls and their bodies; and innumerable others still that are contained in that first chapter, which a keen-sighted man will readily discern and can, if he so desires, dig out. Paul, even taken by himself, seems to me to be as it were a limitless sea of wisdom and piety... I have written this... so that your mind... can see from this sample how much gold there is hidden in Paul.

In 1498, the humanist, Desiderius Erasmus, came to Oxford and, although he and Colet had their disagreements, the two men enjoyed much spiritual fellowship and conversation. Erasmus was struck with his friend's earnestness and power. 'In his voice, his eye, his whole countenance and mien, he seem raised, as it were, out of himself'. Erasmus, however, had not had the same spiritual experience as Colet. For Colet had given up the world of the Schoolmen, having found, in the Scriptures, the Christ – the one whom he now trusted and loved, and whom he wished to serve with the rest of his life. 'Christ had become the ruling passion of his life'.

Meanwhile, the university afforded Colet no official recognition for his work on the Romans nor, in time, on 1 Corinthians. Nor do we know if Colet saw much of the full beneficial effect of his labours. Even so, despite these setbacks, on and on he went with his work, continually casting his bread upon the water, confident that God would bring his labours to fruition in his own good time. The fact is, however, God *was* blessing his work. After Colet had left Oxford, the young theological students, more and more, were turning away from the Schoolmen and exploring the Scriptures for themselves. And included in this number was one William Tyndale.

Some time before 1505, Colet's work at Oxford came to an end when he was appointed doctor, and promoted to be Dean of St Paul's. Here, the field of his labours was widened, and he was able to preach to the people of London, not excluding some who belonged to the Court. And so they, too, as had the students at Oxford, heard the gospel plainly preached from Scripture – not buried under the subtleties of the scholastics.

In 1510, Colet devoted his fortune (he had come into a large inheritance upon the death of his father) to the founding of his school of St Paul's: 'My intent is by this school especially to increase knowledge, and worshipping of God and our Lord Jesus Christ, and good Christian life and manners in the children'.

But he allowed none of this to get in the way of his preaching and other duties as Dean, and the newness of his style, and the warmth and earnestness of his preaching, attracted many. Although Colet himself was no Lollard, in his preaching and his counsel the heretics found much to encourage them. So it is not surprising that in the heresy trials yet to be unleashed, it was easy for the accusers to trace a connection from their victims back to Colet and his preaching.

But it was not simply Paul who had captivated Colet. It was Christ. Erasmus could record that Colet never travelled without reading some book or talking of Christ. And his life matched his discovery of Christ. At home, he dismissed the normal trappings of office, resigned his rich living at Stepney, lived in frugal simplicity, wore plain dress, and was generous. At table, he contrived to engage his guests in serious conversation, after which, gathering his friends around him, they talked of Christ long into the night.

On Friday, February 6th, 1512, Colet had to ascend the pulpit to preach at the opening of the Convocation, called by Henry VIII, in part, for the extirpation of heresy. Colet knew that one of the causes of the increase of heretics, and the rise in heresy, was disgust at the corruption of the Church brought about by the carnality of the very Churchmen before him. The preaching of such a sermon to such a congregation presented him with no easy task.

But Colet was up to the job. He announced his text, Romans 12:2: 'Do not be conformed to this world, but be transformed by the renewing of your mind, that you may prove what is that good and acceptable and perfect will of God'. He had two divisions: 'First, [the apostle] prohibits our being conformed to the world and becoming carnal; and then he commands that we be reformed in the Spirit of God, in order that we may be spiritual'.

Facing his hearers directly, he confronted them with their sin, laying it out in specific detail. In plain language, with no mincing of words, he rebuked their pride, their lust, their

11

covetousness, their worldliness, their hypocrisy. 'Wherefore you fathers, you priests, and all of you of the clergy, awake at length, and rise up from this your sleep in this forgetful world; and being awake, at length listen to Paul calling unto you: "Be not conformed to this world"'.

Turning to the positive, he told his hearers that reformation had to begin with them. We want no new laws, he declared. We have laws enough! It was sin, their sin first of all, that had to be dealt with. And they had to reform themselves:

Claim for yourselves that true liberty of Christ, that spiritual liberty through grace from sin, and serve God and reign in him... As Paul commands: 'Be reformed in the newness of your minds, that you may know the things which are of God; and the peace of God shall be with you!'

Colet's sermon, which so plainly and so pointedly called for repentance and return to God through Christ, reached a much wider public after it had been printed and published in Latin and (probably) English. For preaching such a sermon, he was a marked man, and suffered persecution. For a while he was silenced, but was eventually reinstated, having narrowly avoided execution as a heretic. Erasmus wrote to him, congratulating him that his pulpit was once again open to him, and encouraged Colet to see good in his bitter experience. Through what had happened, he said, the people would be the more eager to hear him – having been deprived of his preaching for a while.

In 1513, Colet preached to Henry himself, and took the opportunity, earnestly and pointedly to direct his remarks against the King's intention to wage war. God protected him in taking this great risk, and the King exacted no revenge. Indeed, Henry retorted: 'Let every one have his own doctor, and let every one favour his own; this man is the doctor for me'.

Colet was appointed preacher for Sunday, November 18th, 1515, at the installation of Thomas Wolsey as Cardinal. Even on this pomp-and-splendour occasion, fraught as it was with danger for the preacher, Colet had the courage to direct his sermon straight at Wolsey – that cruel compound of pride, ambition and love of magnificence and grandeur:

Let not one in so proud a position, made most illustrious by the dignity of such an honour, be puffed up by its greatness. But remember our Saviour, in his own person, said to his disciples: 'I came not to be ministered unto, but to minister'; and: 'He who is least among you shall be the greatest in the kingdom of heaven'; and again: 'He who exalts himself shall be humbled, and he who humbles himself shall be exalted'.

Colet survived three attacks of the sweating sickness (usually fatal within twenty-four hours of its onset), but only at the expense of a shattered constitution. So much so, he finally succumbed to the disease and died on September 16th, 1519. Erasmus wrote: 'He now is safely enjoying Christ, whom he always had upon his lips and at his heart'. Again: 'O true theologian! O wonderful preacher of evangelical doctrine! With what earnest zeal did he drink in the philosophy of Christ! How eagerly did he imbibe the spirit and feelings of... Paul! How did the purity of his whole life correspond to his heavenly doctrine! How many years, following the example of... Paul, did he teach the people without reward!'

* * *

Although, as I have said, I cannot commend Colet in everything, and some of the events of his life remain as paradoxes (or, truth to tell, contradictions) beyond my wit to explain, I cannot help wondering how he would have gone on if he had lived a few more years. It is one of those 'what-ifs?' which, perhaps, we should not ask but, nevertheless, nag at the back of the mind.

What am I talking about? Let us not forget that Erasmus published his Greek New Testament in 1516, and Luther nailed his theses to the door at Wittenberg a year later. Colet died in 1519 – within three years of these momentous events, less than two years after Luther's seemingly little – but, in fact, earth-moving – act which led to the Reformation. Nor must the isolation of those days be forgotten – no internet, no email, no mobile telephone. Information took weeks to travel – not nanoseconds, as today.

But leaving to one side what might have been, and sticking to what we do know of Colet, what lessons can we learn from his life and labours? I believe he has much to teach us and challenge us about today. Much, I say. Speaking for myself, I am moved, confronted and encouraged by what I have learned of John Colet. Let me set out the leading points as they appear to me.

LESSONS FROM COLET'S LIFE AND WORK

I have not produced this small work out of antiquarian interest or as some sort of (very minor) historical account. As I have said, John Colet was above all a preacher. As such, he applied the doctrine of Scripture to his hearers. Well then... I know I have not been expounding Scripture, but in light of Colet's life and work, it would be a travesty to leave the record there. One of the leading reasons for looking at history, surely, is that we should try to draw lessons from the past.

With that in mind, I believe that John Colet 'being dead, still speaks' (Heb. 11:4). I now set out six ways in which he speaks to me – and I hope, reader, to you:

First, in the very worst of times, let us not despair. The days were dark and growing darker when Colet began his work. Islam was conquering the world. Christianity was withering. The Church was decadent and impotent. Well, we today (in the UK at least) have suffered decades of deadening spiritual apathy. And this has sapped us. Furthermore, false doctrine is raising its head in the churches at an alarming rate. In addition, contrary to Colet, many today, who should know better, are turning back to the Fathers. Above all, an assertive, vigorous Islam is, it seems, conquering all before it. The days are dark indeed. Nevertheless, let us learn from Colet, and take courage. Dark as it was when God brought Colet on to the scene, hopeless as it would have seemed, within a few years, the LORD had brought about the Reformation with all its attendant blessings. Colet played his part in that. So let us not despair. God still reigns. He can yet raise men and women to do his will, and bring about better days. Let us trust him. Faith is still the means that God uses in his people to 'subdue kingdoms'. Others before us 'out of weakness were made strong... turned to flight the armies of the aliens' (Heb. 11:33-34). The age of 'these who have turned the world upside down' (Acts 17:6) has not yet come to an end. Christ still says: 'All authority has been given to me in heaven and on earth. Go therefore... and lo, I am with you always, even to the end of the age' (Matt. 28:18-20). Let us, therefore, quit ourselves like men and be strong (see 1 Cor. 16:13, AV), 'be men of courage' (NIV). Let us draw strength from Colet's experience.

Secondly, Colet reminds us that Scripture is one of the two main weapons God has placed in our hand. The other being, of course, prayer. 'The weapons of our warfare are not carnal but mighty through God for the pulling down of strongholds' (2 Cor. 10:4). The followers of Mohammed can and do use the sword. But, in contrast, Christ directly forbids it. He uses his people's prayers and their wielding of 'the sword of the Spirit, which is the word of God' (Eph. 6:17). Scripture is our mighty weapon by the power of the Holy Spirit. So let us learn from Colet. As he rejected the scholasticism of his day, let us turn our back on the worn out philosophies of the age – however new and fancy their dress might be. Let us give up our aping of the world and all its psychological techniques. Let us not go back to the Fathers. Let us return to Scripture. Colet did so, and preached it in its plain sense. And he lived it out in his life. Let us do the same. Let us get back to Scripture. Let us preach Scripture. Let us live it out.

Thirdly, Colet tells us yet again that we must preach the gospel. And I want to stress 'preach'. Colet announced a series of lectures at Oxford. *But he did not lecture.* Oh no! Not at all! *He preached.* And when he left the lectern and got into the pulpit, he continued to preach. We, too often today, announce a sermon, and... what do we do? We lecture! Shame on us! Colet preached, I say. He did not stop with the text. He not only opened up the arguments of Scripture, not only displayed those arguments to the mental satisfaction of his hearers, he went after the people and applied those arguments to them. And he did it with fervour. He was earnest. He was pointed. He was blunt. He was direct. He confronted. He spoke to the very people in front of him. He didn't deal with issues on another planet, or belonging to an age which had long since passed away. Perish the thought! Of course he knew what it is to be afraid. But, paying no regard to their person or power, he communicated with the people who were listening to him at that moment, and dealt with their sins, their hearts, their souls. He went after *them*. He touched them. He set out to change them. And he did it by Scripture. In other words, he preached!

Fourthly, Colet would tell us that Christ is all. Colet found Christ through the Scriptures, principally the letters of Paul. And, having found him, he made much of Christ in his conversation. In private and in public, he preached Christ. So must we. Islam will be stopped, Mohammedans will be converted, ice-like legalism will be melted, the deadening fog of apathy will be lifted, sinners will be saved – only by Christ. Christ must be preached. Christ must be trusted. Christ must be obeyed. Christ is Christianity and Christianity is Christ. 'Christ is all and in all' (Col. 3:11). 'Him we preach' (Col. 1:28). The apostle himself gives us the key: 'I determined not to know anything among you except Jesus Christ and him crucified' (1 Cor. 2:2). What other doctrine could one possibly find when studying the letter to the Romans as Colet did? Badgering Parliament for statutes against an aggressive Islam is worse than useless. Pestering Parliament to pass laws to try to bolster some sort of Christendom is a disaster. Pagans will not be converted in that way! It is the Lord Jesus Christ – the Lord Jesus Christ preached, the Lord Jesus Christ trusted by repentant sinners – *that* is the way. And it is only Christ: 'Nor is there salvation in any other, for there is no other name under heaven given among men by which we must be saved' (Acts 4:12).

Fifthly, let us cultivate true spiritual fellowship. But I mean 'fellowship'! Fellowship does not come out of a coffee jar. It comes from Christ. Christ trusted, Christ loved, Christ talked of, Christ shared. This is spiritual fellowship. Colet did much good by – and, no doubt, received much benefit from – such earnest conversations as he enjoyed with others on the all-important subject, the all-dominating obsession of his life, the one thing needful; namely, Christ.

Sixthly, let us labour on, despite seeming failure, looking to God to bless our labours in his own good time. Colet had this very much in mind. And he took steps to make sure that his work would live on and be a blessing to a rising generation. He did not confine his thinking to his own passing affairs, to his own day. He took the broad sweep. He took the long view. So must we. What of the years to come? What can I do to be a blessing to a generation yet unborn? What can I leave behind me which will do good? How can I, Abel-like, speak good things when I am dead? What crust can I cast on the water for Christ today?

LAST WORDS

Such are the lessons I would draw from the life and labours of John Colet. He may have lived, laboured and died five hundred years ago, but he speaks with a voice we need to hear – and to listen to – today.

As I have indicated, no doubt a very different portrait could have been painted of the man. He had his faults. He made his mistakes. He was a poor sinner like us all. But, speaking for myself, if, after I am dead, somebody can draw six practical lessons for the glory of God out of my life and work, I should be more than pleased.

What about you, reader? The days are dark. There is no denying it. The times are desperate. Let us admit it. There is no hope for us in ourselves. Far from it. Nor will Parliament pull our chestnuts out of the fire. Christendom does not have the solution. It never did. Modern psychological techniques will not do the job. The advocates of user-friendly inclusivism do not have the answer.

But John Colet did. And his answer was Christ, Christ as set forth in Scripture. Principally, Colet found the Christ in the letter to the Romans, and, having found him, having 'dug him out', he preached him. God blessed his labours, and glorified the name of Christ in so doing. And Colet, being long dead, still speaks.

Who knows? God might yet do the same through us and our poor labours in these dark and dying days. Reader, will you through this glance at the life and labours of John Colet, take courage, draw stimulus and receive the challenge to press on and continue to lift up Christ? Do you trust him? Do you love him? Are you determined to serve him?

Me? Me serve Christ? Yes, you! If you are a believer, you are a 'preacher'. Oh, I don't mean you climb up into a pulpit and address a congregation. No! But by your life and lip you are a preacher every day of your life. Or should be! We speak to

19

family, to friend and neighbour. Or should do! After all, we must never forget that 'preaching' is not confined to a pulpit. When the early church was persecuted, the believers were driven out of Jerusalem. 'Those who had been scattered preached the word wherever they went... telling the message... telling them the good news about the Lord Jesus'; that is, they talked to people, they told them about Christ, they 'gossiped' the gospel. And 'the Lord's hand was with them, and a great number of people believed and turned to the Lord' (Acts 8:4; 11:19-21). Furthermore, the life lived should be a witness (1 Pet. 3:1-2,8-17, for instance). All this sort of thing is included in what the New Testament calls 'preaching'. Let me remind you of what Colet said upon the subject: 'At no time, in no place, and in no way, must one be ashamed of the gospel... It is up to the man who knows the right way to point it out to others, and unceasingly summon them back to it'. See also Ezekiel 3:17-21; 33:1-11.

And, reader, if you are not a believer, Colet has a word or two for you. He had surely learned of Paul: 'I am so eager to preach the gospel... I am not ashamed of the gospel, because it is the power of God for the salvation of everyone who believes' (Rom. 1:15-16). He would tell you that the Christ of the gospel is your only hope. The gospel, of course, warns you of the eternal judgement that awaits you for not trusting the Lord Jesus Christ. But, as it also says: 'Everyone who calls on the name of the Lord will be saved' (Rom. 10:13). Call, my reader, call. Repent, turn from your sin, and trust the Lord Jesus – now – and you will be saved.

Finally, turning once again to those of us who have called upon Christ to saved us, it may it be said of us, as Paul could say to the Colossians: 'You serve the Lord Christ' (Col. 3:24). That being so, we should heed the apostle: 'Let us not grow weary while doing good, for in due season we shall reap if we do not lose heart' (Gal. 6:9). 'Therefore, my beloved brethren, be steadfast, immoveable, always abounding in the work of the Lord, knowing that your labour is not in vain in the Lord' (1 Cor. 15:58).

If you have profited by this booklet...

you might like to read about other titles by the same author

Voyage To Freedom

'You are standing on the narrow quay-side waiting to board a small sailing ship. You are about to make an exciting but dangerous and uncomfortable voyage...'

So begins the racy and imaginative account of *The Mayflower* which David Gay has written specially for young people. His exciting historical narrative follows the nine week passage of the pilgrims through the eyes of an imaginary family, Matthew and Martha Lovelace, with their typical children, Justice and Prudence. They encounter such fascinating characters as Master Reynolds, John Howland and William Butten – all of whom really took the Mayflower's historic voyage. Here are three thousand miles of adventure, written with a sensitive appreciation of God's care for his people, and young people's love for adventure.

Christians Grow Old

'A book like this is long overdue. Much has been written for and about the young, but comparatively little about the needs, experiences and contribution of older believers. Based firmly on biblical teaching, this book seeks to rectify the imbalance, and establish the fact that elderly mature Christians should hold a responsible and honoured place in the family and in the church. This should be clearly recognised and acknowledged. What is written here is stimulating, suggestive and searching. Wise words are here, not only for the old, but for us all, whatever our age might be' (Norman R.Perry).

Battle For The Church

1517-1644 were momentous years in the history of the church – from the break with Rome to the rise of the Particular Baptists. David Gay tells the moving story with clarity and passion. In these pages, the main characters are brought vividly to life. Many endured horrific sufferings – hunger, prison, torture and exile. Why? Because they wanted New Testament church life.

But they had powerful enemies – enemies who exacted a price in blood by means of branding iron, stake and hangman's noose. Even so, those believers who 'did not love their lives to the death' took up spiritual arms in the battle for the church. Trusting in God, by his grace they triumphed. This book traces the course of their life-and-death struggle.

But here you have far more than a list of facts. The author, who is a preacher, makes pointed application throughout. You may not always agree with his conclusions, but you will be made to think – and not only about events which took place 400 years ago. Many of today's churches are in a tragic condition, and must be reformed. What lessons can you learn from the past?

Battle For The Church *chronicles the years 1517-1644 in the history of the Church; a time largely forgotten, but a critical period in which multitudes of men, women and children made the supreme sacrifice in their attempt to recapture New Testament church life. Warning! This book contains strong medicine for the church of today which will not be easy to take. But take it we must if the church is ever to recover the spiritual health and vitality it enjoyed in the New Testament era. If you like to be challenged, this book is for you. Highly recommended for [preachers and non-preachers] alike who are willing to continue in the battle for the church* (A review on the internet: 'A book of church history unlike any other you have read', February 15th, 1999).

The Gospel Offer *is* Free

Does God command all sinners to repent and believe?

Does God desire the salvation of all sinners?

Yes, says the Bible, yes to both questions.

But many who love the doctrines of grace are confused. They think God's absolute sovereignty in election, Christ's particular redemption of the elect, and the Holy Spirit's specific application of that redemption to the elect, conflicts with the 'free offer'. It does no such thing! If you doubt it, read this book!

The argument is no trifling matter, no splitting of hairs. The 'free offer' is the biblical way of preaching the gospel. Today, we see the grievous consequences of too-little preaching the gospel as it ought to be preached. 'How the gold has become dim!' (Lam. 4:1). Within these pages, therefore, you will come across no apology for the 'free offer', no mere defence of it. Quite the reverse. You will find that the 'free offer' is a vital part of God's free grace, and that a return to the preaching of it in the biblical way is one of the great needs of the hour.

Gordon Murray: *The argument is based solidly on Scripture and is supported by innumerable quotations from a wide group of preachers and writers. As a demolition job you are hardly likely to find anything more thorough. Yet the book is far more than that. It is even more than an excellent biblical justification for preaching the gospel call freely to all. There is a passion about it that should move all of us who are called to minister the word to others. We know that the work that makes an unbeliever a Christian can only be done through the Holy Spirit, but are our hearts really moved with compassion and the desire that others should come to the Lord? It would be worth reading this book simply to have that impressed on our minds and hearts, but there is far more as well.*

Paul Bevan: *It is certainly a much needed message. First, among those who have developed a 'theology' that is unbiblically restrictive. And, secondly, it is most necessary in the present day Reformed preaching which often tends to 'labour' the gospel and not stress the urgency and the 'now' to repent, believe and trust in Christ. Thank you again for your very relevant book. I trust it will be greatly used by God to encourage preachers in their gospel work.*

Robert Oliver: *It did me good to read it. The subject is so important and you have written so well. The cause of Christ in England has been grievously damaged by the denial of the free offer of the gospel... I pray that God will... make your book useful at home and abroad.*

Aubrey Ridge: *Using economy of expression and abundant sweet reasoning from Scripture, this experienced author pleads for an acceptance of God's word against man's interpretation, to place before us the irrefutable truth:* The Gospel Offer **is** Free... *The book is a treasure that cannot be bettered for value. Do buy it.*

Percival Tanierla: *I am truly encouraged by your clear and scriptural stand. I like your style of writing and the simple English constructions of your sentences. I like your discussions about duty faith,* etc. *I gave a copy to some friends who are sympathetic to the gospel offer. This is to make them more firm and to be encouraged to continue in defending the real faith once delivered to the saints.*

Joe Sheetz: *Your book is being well received... Robert Briggs is very excited about it – says it is the best he has ever read regarding the gospel offer.*

B.A.Ramsbottom: *This is a book with which we do not agree!... [But] we appreciate the courteous way in which Mr Gay has written, and also that he never tries to set up some monster of his own devising – an exaggerated position which no one has ever held or even thought – and then hurl stones at it. Sadly, many have spoiled their arguments by doing this.*

Hugh Collier: *The book... finding it very helpful.*

William Macleod: *Your excellent book. I very much enjoyed reading it and found it gave an excellent readable presentation of the subject.*

Ted Chubb: *Delighted... such a useful volume on such an important and apposite matter... I feel this will be a valuable contribution to the subject – especially in Reformed circles where, sadly, men still look over their shoulders – metaphorically speaking – when preaching the gospel, in case they are accused of too much freedom in the offer of Christ. That is obviously why you wrote this book (among other higher reasons), I am sure, so thank you for a timely publication.*

Iain Murray: *Just a line to thank you heartily for your new book* The Gospel Offer **is** Free. *It is splendid – I have read it all with much appreciation and thankfulness. May it have a wide circulation.*

Bob Gilbert: *I have found it both helpful and challenging 'Who is sufficient?'... I think your book would be valuable as part of [The Preachers' Seminary] as part of their book reading list.*

Trevor Knight: *I have delayed sending my 'thank you'... until I had actually read your book. This I have now done – so herewith my hearty thanks... Those of us who believe 'the gospel offer is free' and endeavour to preach it as such (though I feel personally I fall far short of the 'compassion' element you refer to), are too frequently 'written off' as being of simplistic (if not 'unscriptural') views... It has been refreshing to be reminded of Spurgeon's attitude in particular. Thank you for all your valiant work. May the Lord make your little volume a blessing to others, encouraging many more to 'preach for a verdict'.*

Particular Redemption
and
The Free Offer

The Bible teaches: (i) Christ died only for the elect; (ii) God offers Christ to all.

This looks like a first-class contradiction.

Many think they have found a way to avoid it. Arminians deny the first statement; hyper-Calvinists, the second. But still the Bible teaches both.

Most Calvinists take another route. They use the formula: 'Christ's death – sufficient for all, effective only for the elect'. In this, some follow Moïse Amyraut and say that Christ died provisionally for all, but effectively only for the elect. Others follow John Owen and say that although Christ's death is sufficient for all on account of who he is, nevertheless it was intended and effective only for the elect. In this way, both think they justify the free offer in light of particular redemption. But both are wrong.

The Bible does not try to solve the seeming paradox. It never uses 'the sufficiency formula'. It simply states that Christ died for the elect, but even so it commands all sinners to repent and believe – promising them Christ and salvation if they do.

While this book does not promise an easy read, it will repay careful study. And the subject is worthy of such. Above all, its author's aim is to glorify God by stimulating the wider, more passionate, and less-inhibited preaching of the free offer to sinners by those who rightly hold to particular redemption.

Michael Haykin: 'Impressive in its discussion of theological perspectives and fully competent in its handling of Scripture, here is an excellent resource for thinking through the nature of biblical evangelism and how it relates to the scriptural theme of the sovereignty of God in salvation, especially as the latter relates to the death of Christ. May those who are tempted to cool their passion for the salvation of sinners in light of convictions about Christ's redeeming work read this book and have that passion re-ignited by the fiery light of God's truth'.

Infant Baptism Tested

This book will not appeal to every Christian.

It is, after all, a polemical work, designed to explore infant baptism and expose it as destructive of the gospel. And it raises important questions: What is a Christian? How does one become a Christian? What is a church? How does one become a member? And, above all, what of the eternal consequences of baby-sprinkling in the name of Christ?

Some believers don't like controversy, full stop. So they won't like this book. Some will deplore its appearance, thinking it divisive in an age of 'togetherness'. Others will consider it a sterile work, opening old wounds, fighting worn-out battles of an age long since gone.

David Gay disagrees. The issue is not dead. Sacramentalism is on the rise in Reformed circles, and elsewhere. Calvin's (and Augustine's) views on infant baptism (and the Lord's supper) are increasingly being turned to. Attitudes to children, and ways of treating them spiritually, are being radically changed on such a basis. And Gay, deploring this, wishes to warn those who are thinking of adopting the Reformer's teaching on infant baptism. Some Baptists, who rightly take the Reformed view of salvation, beguiled by the names of the 'big guns' who baptise infants, are attracted by the seeming logic of 'covenant theology'. 'Look before you leap', is Gay's theme.

To help such readers take a good look *before* they leap, and to challenge those who already baptise infants, he has produced this book – which does what it says in the title: *Infant Baptism Tested*.

So, reader, if you think it right to contend earnestly for the faith, and if, with an open Bible, you are prepared to examine infant baptism, and willing to test its practice, and thus come to an informed decision about it, this book is for you. If, after reading it, you don't agree with the author, at least you will have thought it all out. But you never know – you might find the seeming heavy-weight arguments put forward by infant baptisers don't stand scriptural scrutiny, that covenant theology is not biblical after all, and that sacramentalism is an abomination.

Are you willing to take that risk?

'I never knew of this author before I read this book so my review is not biased. I was raised in the Reformed tradition (CRC and then URC churches) so I always just accepted infant baptism and my bubble of a worldview. I recently met a Reformed Baptist Christian who told me about how unbiblical infant baptism is – so I read and studied as many books as I could about the subject – which left me very confused (four years of reading and praying) – until I bought this little known book or author (no offense David Gay). Let all readers see this review and let me tell ALL that this is a book that shook me (in a good way) and changed the way I read God's word and what I believed and this book is quite amazing – David Gay has many footnotes (many!!!) that back up what he writes and many quotes and this book is laid out in quite a organized manner that takes the reader down the biblical path of truth – (I kicked and screamed the whole time I was led down the path) – this book shows the history of infant baptism and the biblical worldview of why infant baptism is wrong and how it leads to confusion about identity and one's own conversion (am I saved or just deluded?). This book is a must for Christians who believe in infant baptism and Christians who don't believe in infant baptism so you witness the truth to those "Christians" who are blind and following blind guides. This book is great – 10 out 10 – easy!' (A review on the internet: 'The book on infant baptism – biblical or not?', July 17th 2010; I have left the American spelling).

Septimus Sears:
A Victorian Injustice and Its Aftermath

Septimus who? Septimus Sears? *Never heard of him*! Such, perhaps, will be the response of many when first hearing of this book. But this good man is worth knowing, and David Gay wants to tell others about him. Some, of course, will know all about him already – or will they? Gay hopes to shine a little light on a particular aspect of Sears' life and work, a light which might help lift the fog of misunderstanding and misrepresentation which has shrouded his memory. More important, in so doing, Gay hopes to bring out some valuable lessons for us today.

An English Victorian (1819-1877), Septimus Sears was the preacher in the Strict Baptist church, Clifton, Bedfordshire, for 35 years. What labours, and what blessing attended his ministry! A man mightily used by God in his generation, he deserves to be better known; he was, simply, one 'of whom the world was not worthy' (Heb. 11:38).

Sadly, however, he was hindered by his hyper-Calvinism. Although he changed his views somewhat, even when he did get closer to biblical freeness in addressing sinners, Sears never managed to throw off the shackles of hyperism. Even so, he was wrongly and bitterly attacked by (principally) John Gadsby in the *Gospel Standard* for being too free with sinners! Moreover, this false accusation was then embodied in additions to the Gospel Standard Articles – unchanged to this day.

Although some want to let this episode sink further and further into oblivion, Gay is convinced that it is a tale which needs telling. Why? Certainly, not to pick over old sores! But, since the lessons of this Victorian injustice serve as a warning to us of the way in which hyper-Calvinism stifles gospel preaching, the facts must come out.

This slim volume is the substance of the paper David Gay read at the annual meeting of the Strict Baptist Historical Society in March 2009. As such, it represents only work in progress. In due course he hopes to publish a fully-detailed book on the subject.

Baptist Sacramentalism

Who would have thought it? I, for one, didn't. It never crossed my mind that it might happen. It really didn't. But I was wrong. It has.

*What has? Baptist sacramentalism! It never occurred to me that Baptists would become sacramentalists. I thought the two were mutually exclusive, self-contradictory. But I was wrong. A growing number of Baptists **are** becoming sacramentalists. Baptist writers are publishing book after book promoting sacramentalism. Baptist teachers are teaching it. Baptist preachers are preaching it. And more and more Baptists are adopting it. I'll say it again. Baptists are becoming sacramentalists! Incredible!*

Wait a minute! Baptist sacramentalism? What are you talking about?

Baptists are convinced that Scripture teaches that those who give a credible profession of saving faith in Christ should be immersed in water – as a public sign or outward symbol of the inward work of God's grace that they have already experienced. Baptists are opposed to sacramentalism. They cannot abide it! Well, that's how things stood until recently. But a growing number of Baptists are now beginning to teach that grace – that the Holy Spirit himself – is actually conveyed to those whom they baptise. Incredible!

Sacramentalism, of course, has long held sway among infant baptisers. In my Infant Baptism Tested, *I exposed it and probed its dreadful consequences. Now I must do the same for Baptist sacramentalism. Hence this book.*

In these pages, I expose what has gone into this Baptist sacramentalism – the re-writing of history, the faulty exegesis of Scripture, and the heady (and poisonous) mixture of ecumenism (including Rome, the Orthodox, eastern religions – not excluding Islam), the charismatic movement, the New Perspective, the re-definition of conversion, and the acceptance of infant baptism. This is what makes up this pernicious cocktail. And it has only one end – baptismal regeneration.

So writes David Gay. If you are a Baptist, he has produced this book to warn you of what, if it has not already done so, is about to hit a seminary, a bookshop or a pulpit near you – and do so very soon. If you are a Baptist who is thinking of adopting this sacramentalism, he wants to let you know what you are in for. Don't buy a pig in a poke! And if you are a Baptist sacramentalist, he wants to challenge the basis of your position and, at the very least, make you question it.

Why does he make such a song and dance about it? Because the consequences are dreadful. If Baptist sacramentalism wins the day, multitudes will be misled into thinking they are saved when they are not. And the consequences of *that* are unthinkable.

The Priesthood of All Believers

'The priesthood of all believers' is a biblical doctrine. Sadly, Satan has laid his meddling fingers on this glorious gospel principle and twisted it to the ruin of many.

How? For a start, the overwhelming majority of believers, for all practical purposes, believe in *the priesthood of **no** believers*. Oh, I know we frequently parrot the phrase 'the priesthood of all believers', and, of course, it features in most of our Confessions of Faith: 'We believe in the priesthood of all believers'. Oh, yes. But too often it has become a mere slogan, a mantra. A form of words without real content or implication, it makes no practical difference to most of us whatsoever. The result is tragic. 'The priesthood of all believers' is a neglected, poor relation of the Christian religion, rarely discussed, let alone thought about, least of all acted upon. Alas, 'the priesthood of *no* believers' is the reality for many.

It gets worse. Worse? Yes, indeed. Millions really believe in *the priesthood of **some** believers*. The truth is, where this is so, in each church it has become *the priesthood of **one** believer*! Really? Yes, for millions – adherents of the Church of Rome and the Church of England, chief among them. But not only they! No, indeed! Most evangelicals (not excluding the Reformed) hold to the priesthood of *some* believers. Oh, yes they do!

And all the time, the New Testament teaches *the priesthood of **all** believers*.

David Gay has written this small work to help believers avoid a trap they often seem to fall into. What 'trap' is that? Gay wants us (he includes himself!) to stop intoning the phrase 'the priesthood of all believers', and then, having touched our cap at it, carrying on as though it meant nothing at all. In short, he wants us to use the phrase, understand what it means, *and then live it out in daily experience*.

The Pastor: Does He Exist?

News headline: 'Humpty Dumpty Strikes Again!'. What's that? 'Humpty Dumpty Strikes Again – in the Church!'. Let me re-phrase it: *Believers Sustain Big Losses by Changing the Meaning of Bible Words.*

Alice was confused. Humpty Dumpty explained: 'When I use a word', he said, 'it means just what I choose it to mean; neither more nor less'. Ah, that makes it clear!

Does it?

When Humpty Dumpty gets to work on a Bible word, trouble always follows – and with a capital 'T'. Sad to say, Humpty Dumpty has been very busy these past two thousand years, and many Bible words have suffered at his hand. Much harm has resulted.

In this book, the words David Gay has in mind are *pastor*, *minister*, *clergy* and *ordain*. Good Bible words, all of them. But did you realise that the overwhelming majority of Christians don't use these Bible words the way the Bible does? Rather, they use them the way Humpty Dumpty invented for them.

Oh, Humpty Dumpty didn't do it himself. No. He used some very learnèd and clever gentlemen to do the job for him – the Fathers. And a proper thorough job they made of it, too. Moreover, their followers are still at it. Indeed, many who ought to know better are driving headlong back to the Fathers. Yes, they are!

What did the Fathers do? Why did they do it? And where have we ended up? What have we lost? Who is carrying on their work to this very day?

Why not read David Gay's book and find out? Why not find out if Humpty Dumpty has misled *you*? Why not find out if he has robbed *you* of some biblical truths and practices?

Christ is All: No Sanctification by the Law

John Calvin inherited the doctrines of the medieval Roman Church. In particular, he inherited that Church's view of the law of God, given to Israel through Moses on Sinai. Calvin took the Church's teaching on this, as it had been developed by Thomas Aquinas, and tweaked it to produce a Reformed threefold-use of the law in the new covenant. Some Anabaptists and others resisted him at the time, but they were heavily out-gunned, and Calvin's system has dominated the Reformed and evangelical world ever since. Millions, who have never read a word of Calvin, many of whom would shudder at the very mention of his name, nevertheless, are, on the law, Calvinists – even though they may not know it.

David Gay contends that Calvin was wrong on the law, and this has had serious consequences. Gay is concerned, in particular, with the Reformer's third use of the law – which is, said Calvin, to sanctify the believer. Gay disagrees. In this book, he probes Calvin's system, exposes it to the light of Scripture, and shows where it departs from the New Testament. He also demonstrates the utter inadequacy of the escape routes used by the Reformed to get round awkward passages of Scripture.

Turning from the negative, Gay then looks at every major New Testament passage dealing with the believer and the law. Next, he sets out scriptural teaching on the true way of sanctification for the believer. This, he shows, is not by the law of Moses; rather, it is by the law of Christ in the hands of the Holy Spirit. Indeed, as Gay makes clear, the law of Christ is, ultimately, Christ himself. Hence his chosen title: *Christ is All*. Having set out the believer's rule, he then answers seven objections levelled against it.

Gay does not pretend that this book is an easy read. But he hopes it will prove a profitable read. And even if others do not agree with him on every point, until they have read what he has to say, it can hardly be fair, can it, to dismiss him out of hand as an antinomian?

Printed in Germany
by Amazon Distribution
GmbH, Leipzig